Saving Trees by Using Science

by Pamela Dell

Scott Foresman
is an imprint of

PEARSON

Glenview, Illinois • Boston, Massachusetts • Chandler, Arizona
Upper Saddle River, New Jersey

Illustrator
Dan Trush

Photographs
Every effort has been made to secure permission and provide appropriate credit for photographic material. The publisher deeply regrets any omission and pledges to correct errors called to its attention in subsequent editions.
Unless otherwise acknowledged, all photographs are the property of Pearson Education, Inc.
Photo locators denoted as follows: Top (T), Center (C), Bottom (B), Left (L), Right (R), Background (Bkgd)

ISBN 13: 978-0-328-51655-1
ISBN 10:   0-328-51655-4

4 5 6 7 8 9 10 V0FL 15 14 13 12 11

Earth's Life-Giving Forests

Imagine our beautiful blue planet with no trees. What would life be like without millions of acres of **untamed** forests? You might answer that the world would be a bare, empty, and **unnatural** place to live. But the problem is much greater than that.

Even from space, Earth's many acres of green forest are visible.

In fact, if there were no trees or other plants, life as we know it couldn't exist at all. Trees give us oxygen—the air we breathe. Without oxygen, we couldn't survive. In fact, all animals would die without the oxygen that trees give off.

Winter in the forestlands of Russia

Spring arrives in Stony Brook, New York.

Autumn woods in Ontario, Canada

It's always like summer in the Brazilian rain forest.

Luckily, billions of trees grow throughout the world. The United States alone has about 755 million acres of forest land. In fact, the United States is one of the four most forest-rich countries in the world. Only Brazil, Russia, and Canada have more land covered by forests.

Trees in Danger

The good news is that there are still many forests in the world. Better still, new trees are growing all the time. But the bad news is very bad. A huge amount of forestland continues to disappear every year.

To address this problem, scientists are working to understand how and why trees are being destroyed. They know that trees face danger from many sources. Human activity is the greatest factor.

As these maps show, our country has lost most of its trees. The green areas show how forested areas have changed.

Areas of Virgin Forest, 1850

0   200 400 miles

Areas of Virgin Forest, 1992

0   200 400 miles

5

Logging

The demand for wood, or lumber, is great throughout the world. In the past, as now, people used lumber for paper, homes, furniture, boats, musical instruments, flooring, and hundreds of other things. But today, the desire for lumber is much greater than it has ever been. Why? The world's population is larger, so there are more people who need or want these products made from wood. Lumber companies work around the clock to meet the demand for wood products that people want. Loggers, who are also called **lumberjacks**, sometimes clear-cut acres of trees at a time. The trees are then sent to lumber mills. Farmers also use this clear-cutting method to remove trees from their land. Then they use the completely cleared land to grow crops and raise herds of animals.

Some logging companies are using more environmentally conscious harvesting techniques.

Out-of-control forest fires are a great danger to animals, trees, and human life.

Other Threats to Forests

Humans are not the only threat to trees. Fire, plant diseases, and some insects are three additional threats. All of these destroy countless trees every year.

Studies show that forest fires have been on the increase recently. Millions of acres burn each year. People sometimes start the fires that destroy forest land. But fires often start naturally too.

Diseases also do a lot of damage to trees. One terrible tree-killer is known as sudden oak death. This disease seems to spread the same way human diseases do—from tree to tree. Many different types of trees can be infected. Unfortunately, sudden oak death has killed more than a million American trees in the past few years.

Insects also can pose a serious threat. In the United States, ash borers, spruce budworms, and certain kinds of pine beetles are a few of the many deadly insect enemies of trees. In some cases, insects destroy acres and acres of forests. They can also kill many much-needed trees in America's cities and suburbs.

This picture shows where sudden oak death has set in.

The emerald ash borer, pictured here, is one of many insects that can kill trees.

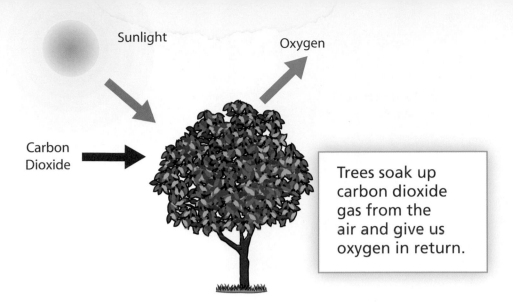

Sunlight

Oxygen

Carbon Dioxide

Trees soak up carbon dioxide gas from the air and give us oxygen in return.

The Importance of Trees

The loss of so many trees is a serious problem for several reasons. What would we do without the wood, paper, medicine, and fruit that come from trees? We all enjoy the shade that trees provide as well.

But perhaps the most important thing that trees do for us has to do with the air that is all around us. You already know that trees provide Earth with oxygen. Scientists also know that trees help keep our air clean by soaking up carbon dioxide.

Carbon dioxide is a gas that cars and other machines spread into the air. When there are not enough trees to absorb all the carbon dioxide, it builds up. And too much carbon dioxide in the air causes temperatures to rise. This build-up is part of the effect known as global warming. Today, people all over the world are beginning to understand the dangers of global warming.

If too much of Earth's ice melts, the effect will be disastrous for all living things.

Global warming affects every part of the world. As temperatures rise, the frozen polar ice caps begin to **thaw**. This melting will add more water to the oceans and perhaps cause flooding on coastal lands. In other areas, a lack of water will create droughts.

One of the many **requirements** for reducing global warming is having thriving forests. So scientists are paying a lot of attention these days to keeping trees alive and healthy. They hope to **harness** the threat of global warming by saving trees.

Science at Work

Silviculture (SILL-va-kull-chur) is the science of growing trees and taking care of them. Scientists in this area—silviculturists—work in many different parts of the world and study different types of trees. But they all share one **feature**. They all care deeply about keeping the world's forests healthy.

Tree scientists are working hard to find ways to improve the growth of existing trees. They watch over the growth of new trees. And they carefully monitor harvesting trees from the Earth's forests so that the forests aren't destroyed.

Some tree scientists work on tree farms like this one (below). Others work in the field, meaning they work on projects in naturally growing forests (right).

Cutting brush and removing dead plants to lessen the risk of accidental fire is another important task. To help prevent even larger outbreaks of fire, foresters may purposely start fires. But they and others carefully watch such controlled fires.

Controlled burning of forestlands is healthy for trees.

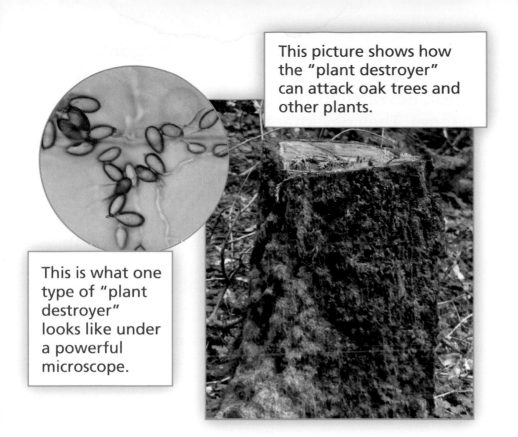

This picture shows how the "plant destroyer" can attack oak trees and other plants.

This is what one type of "plant destroyer" looks like under a powerful microscope.

Progress is being made in fighting tree diseases too. In 2006, a group of scientists studying these diseases made a public **announcement**. They had discovered some important information about a group of deadly plant killers. These killers are called *phytophthora* (fy-TOFF-thor-uh), or "plant destroyers." One type of these tiny, funguslike destroyers is the cause of sudden oak death.

What the scientists learned will help them find treatments for tree diseases that are caused by the plant destroyers. They may even discover ways to get rid of these diseases altogether!

Another study is taking place in Oregon's Cascade Mountains at the Andrews Experimental Forest. Researchers there record all of the forest's changes. They pay attention to how changes in climate, or the long-term weather, affect the forest. They also monitor how the trees respond to other changes in the environment. What they learn at this research forest will be valuable in protecting this forest and other forests on Earth.

A scene from Andrews Experimental Forest in Oregon

From North America to Asia, children are helping to plant trees. American students plant a tree in Iowa (left), and Filipino students plant a tree in Manila (below).

Around the globe, scientists are trying new and different ways to save Earth's trees. They are gaining more knowledge about trees and forest health all the time. But it's not only scientists who can help protect forests. We all can help save our world's beautiful and very important forests! By simply planting a tree—and by recycling paper and other products made from lumber—we all can make a big difference.

Glossary

announcement *n.* act of announcing or making known

feature *n.* a distinct part or quality

harness *v.* to control and put to use

lumberjacks *n.* people whose work is cutting down trees

requirements *n.* things that are needed

thaw *v.* to melt ice, snow, or anything frozen

unnatural *adj.* not natural; not normal

untamed *adj.* wild; not obedient